P9-CEL-979

This book was written and illustrated by a friend XX went to school with when she was growing up.

Pappa and XX anxiously await and look forward to your arrival and can't wait to read this to you!

OXOXOX 2015

Christmas

Welcome to the World!
With Magical Wishes,

McHORN
AND HIS HIDDEN SPOTS

Laura Seeley

This book is dedicated to CLINT and GAIL, my parents.
One I dearly miss; one I dearly cherish. They are the source of my own spots.

With much appreciation to Barry Berg/B2 Productions.
With gratitude to Anne Mercer Larson, enhancer and editor.
And with thanks to Mary McKay, Scott E. Sutton, Dee Lundell and Dana Yarger.

McHORN. AND HIS HIDDEN SPOTS.
Text and illustrations copyright © 2015 Laura Seeley. All rights reserved.
No part of this book may be used or reproduced in whole or in part or stored in a retrieval system or transmitted
in any form or by any means electronic, mechanical, photocopying, recording or otherwise without
written permission of the publisher, except in the case of brief quotations embodied in critical reviews and articles.
Inquiries regarding permissions should be addressed to the publisher.

ISBN 978-0-9864250-0-4

Published by

BEST FRIENDS ART GALLERY
Dana Point, California

www.LauraSeeley.com and www.BestFriendsArtGallery.com
https://www.facebook.com/pages/LAURA-SEELEY-STUDIO/192163102682

McHORN
AND HIS HIDDEN SPOTS

Words and Pictures by

Laura Seeley

BEST FRIENDS  ART GALLERY

McHorn, the Dalmatian, a spotted creation,
would boast that his spots made him best.
"I'm the number one creature because of this feature.
You ALL should be very impressed."

The other dogs scoffed at the spotted show-off,
who felt sure he was second to none.
Then they all ran away for their puppy dog play...

Around HIM they just didn't
have fun.

But the uppity pup kept his nose pointed up,
quite convinced he was meant to be boss.
"Silly doggies!" he howled.
"They're just jealous," he growled.
Either way it was clearly
THEIR loss.

He was terribly fond of a spot by the pond,
where he loved to observe his reflection.
With EACH look he knew that it really was true...
He was painfully close to perfection.

Past the pond up the hill,
his big project and thrill,
was a secret that no one could see.
Any THING polka-dotted
or speckled or spotted,
he stuffed in this old hollow tree.

He had one thing in mind-
to be king of his kind.
"I'm the SPOT king, I am!"
thought the hound.
Other things that had spots
tied his stomach in knots.
So he stashed every spot
that he found.

Then along came the day,
to his dappled dismay,
when he found in his house
a surprise.
What a sickening sight!
IT WAS SPOTTED AND WHITE!
And it watched him
with black button eyes.

"Another Dalmatian?"
he thought with frustration.
"Now IT will get all
the attention!
This simply can't be!
It looks TOO much like me!"
And he barked
at this spotted invention.

It didn't bark back. And it didn't attack.
It just stared with those black button eyes.
So he sniffed at its fur but it still wouldn't stir
and McHorn felt his blood pressure rise.

On the spotted thing's head
was a ribbon bright red
neatly tied in a beautiful bow.
Now he REALLY was mad.
That was MORE than he had...

THIS DOG-THING WITH SPOTS
HAD TO GO!

This was true spotted war
and he dashed through the door
with a fearless and firm puppy grip,
taking care as he trotted
that nobody spotted
his button-eyed dog-stealing trip.

He snuck past the pond
to the tree just beyond
where he'd hidden that polka-dot pile.
"Now NO ONE will see!"
thought the puppy with glee
and he tossed it right in
with a smile.

He stretched and he sighed,
feeling quite satisfied
and decided to snooze for a while.
He would stay the spot king
and no spotted DOG thing
would be cramping
his slick puppy style.

What a frightening dream!
What a fur-raising scene
about taking a bath in a pail...

SPOT REMOVER

All that bubbly fluff
had been
spot-cleaning
stuff
and had washed
off his spots
HEAD
to
TAIL!

What a nightmarish sight,
all that plain puppy white!
And he ran toward the pond,
very worried.
Feeling quite insecure,
he just had to be sure
that he still had his spots,
SO HE HURRIED!

With eager inspection
he found his reflection.
HIS SPOTS WERE STILL THERE!
And he sighed.
But his sigh of relief
was remarkably brief
and his puppy eyes
OPENED UP WIDE...

First, he spotted a duck and a wading woodchuck
that were covered with speckles and spots.
There were spots on a skunk and a chewing chipmunk
and his tummy got tied up in knots.

"A polka-dot bird?
This is simply absurd!"
thought McHorn as he fought off the jitters.
"And four spotted fish? This is just devilish!
HOW ON EARTH CAN I HIDE
ALL THESE CRITTERS?"

There were more on a moose
and a fox and a goose
and a bunch on the back of a bear.
Speckled critters galore!
Spotted beasts by the score!
What a number one
NASTY NIGHTMARE!

The spotted dognapper who'd once felt so dapper
looked down at his spots with a whine.
NOW what would he do? All the rest had them, too,
and now spots didn't seem all that fine!

His puppy head ached. How much more could he take?
Was this still some ridiculous dream?
Or a dreadful pay-back for his polka-dot stack
and his button-eyed dognapping scheme?

Then he hollered
A HOWL
as a huge spotted owl
snatched him up
and he thought
he'd be swallowed!

While his puppy nerves JUMPED
and his puppy heart THUMPED
they flew OFF to the tree
that was hollowed.

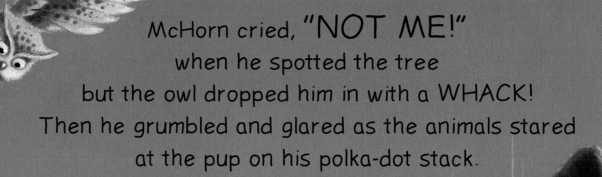

McHorn cried, "NOT ME!"
when he spotted the tree
but the owl dropped him in with a WHACK!
Then he grumbled and glared as the animals stared
at the pup on his polka-dot stack.

"What a shameful display
to be treated this way!"
thought McHorn
as he sat with a scowl.
"I'm supposed to be great,
not some spotted BIRD bait
for an IMPOLITE

OVERSIZED

OWL!"

What a bullying bird!
But then
something occurred
to the pup
and he felt like a fool.

Hadn't HE
done the SAME
in his
SPOT- HIDING game?

Acting SNEAKY?
And NAUGHTY?
And CRUEL?

Just under his chin
was his little stuffed twin
and it seemed to observe him
unblinking.

So timid and teeny.
He'd been such a meany!
How COULD he have been
so unthinking?

He felt strange underneath,
even UGLY beneath all his spots,
and his thoughts became scattered.

Underneath he felt bad. Underneath he felt sad.

Could the underneath part
BE WHAT MATTERED?

McHorn felt like crying
but spots started flying

a r o u n d

and around

and around . . .

...then he tumbled and twirled
in a spot-flooded world
full of critters and things
he had found.

"HELP ME!
I'M FALLING!"
McHorn began calling.
"CAN ANYONE HEAR ME?
PLEASE HELP!"

The owl screeched "HOO!"
Then he heard something "MOO",
and he burst wide awake
with a YELP.

He opened his eyes
as a face of great size
LOWERED
DOWN
for a close-up inspection.

His heartbeat still raced
as she moved towards his face...
Then she licked him
with spotted affection.

In a world full of spots there would always be lots
and McHorn finally figured this out.
Though he felt pretty small he was part of it all.
Could it be that's what life was about?

He would think of his blunder
and sometimes he'd wonder
just WHAT he had done it all for...
an immense revelation
for one young Dalmatian,
a bit more grown-up than before.

The stuff in the stack? Well, he took it all back.
Hiding spots was no LONGER much fun.
With more HEART and less PRIDE he felt better inside,
knowing spot wars could never be won.

He got used to his part in this spot-sharing art.
This was now the NEW pledge he was keeping,
(though he still felt some knots, teeny-weeny sized knots
when he noticed a ladybug creeping).

And McHorn never knew something spotted and blue
had been laid in the old hollow tree...
just the place for providing and perfect for hiding

a secret or two...

even three.

OTHER BOOKS WRITTEN and ILLUSTRATED by LAURA SEELEY

THE BOOK OF SHADOWBOXES, A Story of the ABCs*

THE MAGICAL MOONBALLS*

JEROME, A Bumpy Journey to Joy

SHADOWBOX HUNT, A Search & Find Odyssey, for ages 5 to 105!

OTHER BOOKS ILLUSTRATED by LAURA SEELEY

AGATHA'S FEATHERBED, Not Just Another Wild Goose Story, by Carmen Deedy*
(Available in both English and Spanish versions)

Tom T. Hall's CHRISTMAS AND THE OLD HOUSE

CATS VANISH SLOWLY, by Ruth Tiller

THE FOUR-LEGGED GHOSTS, by Mary Hoffman

THE LEMON LOVER'S COOKBOOK, by Peg Bailey

THE BOY OF STEEL, by Ray Negron

THE GREATEST STORY NEVER TOLD, by Ray Negron

ONE LAST TIME, by Ray Negron

C.C.CLAUS, A Baseball Christmas Story, by C.C. Sabathia and Ray Negron

*ALSO AVAILABLE IN SOFT COVER.